CW01582920

ANIMAL
Activity Book

ALAIN GRÉE

Button Books

Flower fun

Which butterfly will land on which flower? Follow the tangled lines to find out.

Spot the difference

Can you spot five differences between these two pictures?

Monkey business

Help the monkey swing through the trees to find the bananas!

Under the sea

Add some stickers to bring this ocean scene to life.

Down at the farm

Can you find these farmyard friends in the puzzle?

a	b	a	l	m	e	r	c	f	h	f	x
m	t	t	g	h	o	r	s	e	e	q	r
p	b	u	l	l	n	l	f	s	n	u	a
i	j	r	o	h	q	g	j	t	y	d	b
g	n	k	c	i	y	u	m	r	p	o	b
l	g	e	o	c	b	v	u	o	h	n	i
e	m	y	w	k	k	t	n	n	w	k	t
t	o	u	t	s	h	e	e	p	n	e	h
y	l	m	s	t	y	n	m	u	s	y	i
z	n	d	x	l	p	a	u	t	i	l	d
r	p	k	o	e	m	l	o	e	c	e	s
m	g	o	a	t	s	p	w	h	d	h	b

bull
cow
donkey
goat
hen
horse
pig
rabbit
sheep
turkey

Hunt the chicks

Find the hidden chicks.
How many can you see?

Beautiful butterflies

Copy the pattern from the butterfly on the left onto the one on the right, then colour it in.

Bird buddies

Here are three different types of bird. Can you put them into groups?
In one group, a bird has a different coloured wing. Which bird is it?

Gone fishing

What is Polly trying to catch? Follow the tangled line to find out.

Colourful coats

On cold, wet or windy days, dogs need more than their own fur to stay warm. Help these dogs to stand out from the crowd by colouring in their coats.

Disappearing act

This owl is disappearing! Complete the picture then colour it in so he can join his friends in the tree.

Quick, quick, slow!

Choose words from the sticker pages to finish this story.

"Ha, ha, ha, you can't catch me! I'm the ______ animal you'll ever see!"

______ the hare. "Prove it," said the tortoise. "I challenge you to a race."

"OK, slowcoach," said the hare. "Last one to finish buys the ______."

So off they went. The hare ______ along, going as fast as he could.

After a while, he became ______ and stopped for a ______.

Meanwhile, the tortoise ______ along, until she reached the finish line.

The hare woke up, only to ______

that the tortoise had beaten him!

Duck colouring fun

Colour in this picture of a duck.

Find the eggs

This magpie has lost her eggs. Can you help her find them?
Write down the number of eggs you have found.

[ ] eggs

Odd one out

Which camel has a different blanket?

Seal surprise

Follow these steps to draw a seal and then colour him in.

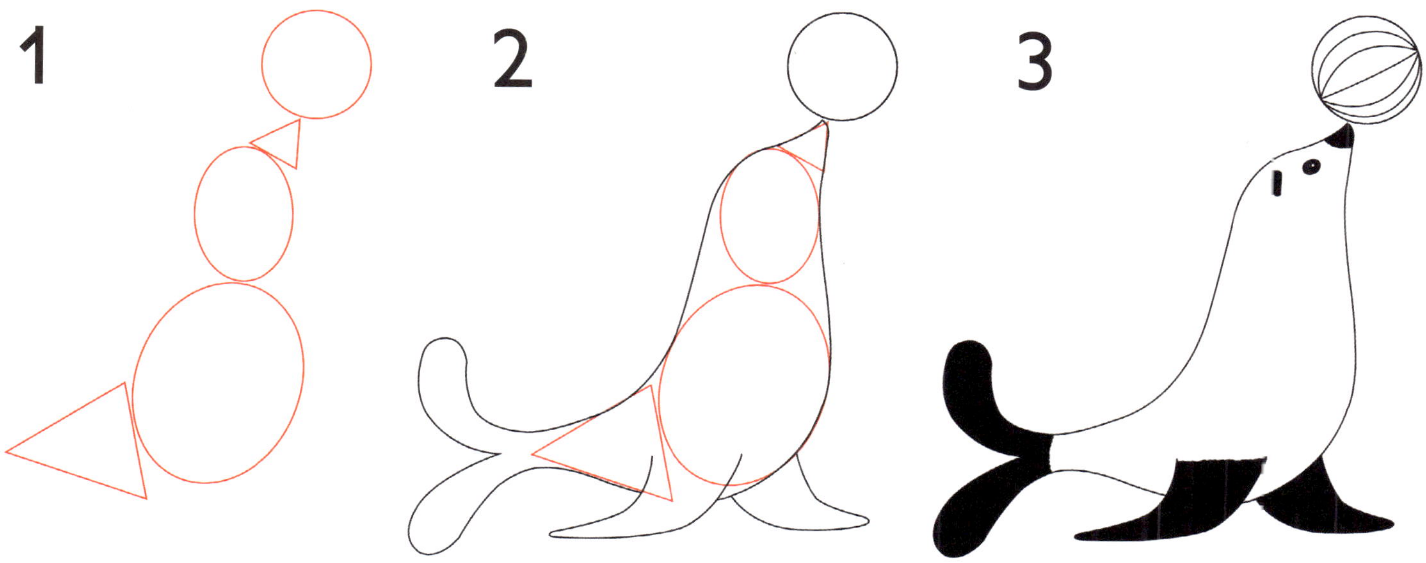

Animal counting

How many animals are in each box? How many animals are there altogether?

Rabbit disguise

To make a bunny face mask, trace this image onto a piece of thin card and colour it in. Poke holes in each side, thread a piece of elastic through them and adjust the elastic to fit.

Hidden insects

Can you help Jack and Polly catch the bugs hiding in this picture?
Draw a circle around each one that you find.

Animal quackers

How many yellow ducks can you find in this picture? How many white ducks are there?
What is the total number of ducks in this picture?

Feline friendly

The lion and tiger want some friends to play with. Can you draw another lion and tiger? You can add some stickers too.

Jump start

Can you help this rider jump the fence correctly by putting these pictures in the right order? Write the numbers in the circles – numbers 1 and 6 have been done for you.

In which picture is the rider wearing a different coloured hat?

1

Start

6

Finish

Find the hens

These chicks are so busy eating, they have lost their mothers! See if you can find out which chick belongs to which hen by following the lines.

Spot the difference

Can you spot five differences between these two pictures?

Off on holiday

Check Romeo the dog's list and work out what's missing from this picture.
Then circle any items in the picture that aren't on his list.

Parasol
Fishing net
Spade
Rubber ring
Shirts
Flipper
Book
Towels
Rug
Bucket

Fishy friends

Can you find all the words in the puzzle?

sole
swordfish
tuna
carp
shark
mackerel
guppy
salmon
trout
cod

s	a	s	h	a	r	k	w	n	m	m	o
w	m	u	z	g	h	j	m	v	a	t	t
o	s	a	l	m	o	n	p	p	c	m	r
r	o	k	m	o	a	q	t	j	k	y	o
d	l	e	w	c	l	y	u	m	e	p	u
f	e	t	f	o	m	b	n	u	r	h	t
i	t	m	v	d	o	k	a	n	e	w	c
s	e	g	u	p	p	y	e	a	l	n	h
h	y	o	m	s	t	y	n	m	u	s	m
z	n	d	x	l	p	a	c	a	r	p	d

Ocean adventure

Add some stickers to bring this ocean scene to life.

Animal halves

These animals have been split in two! Use the stickers to put them back together again.

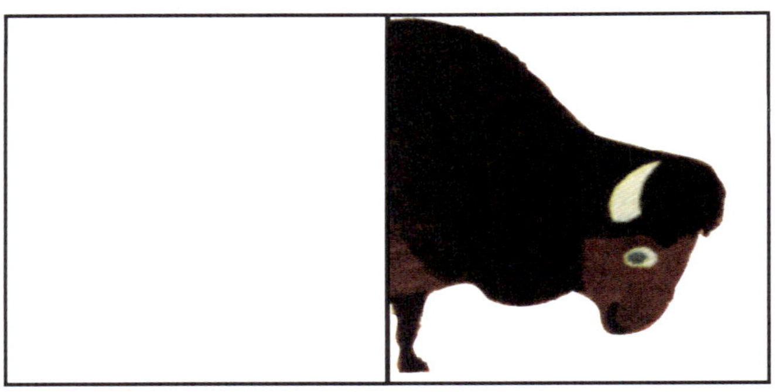

All muddled up

This parrot has got her animal friends' names jumbled up. Can you help her work out what she wants to say?

toga

okoranag

macel

tuvlure

Tangled lines

Can you work out what each of these elephants wants to eat?

Forest friends

How many animals can you see?
Which do you think is the slowest?

Animal race

Starting at the snake, take turns to throw a dice with a friend and see who is the first to reach the fox. If you land on a sun, you get an extra go!

Jungle pals

Can you find all these jungle animals in the puzzle?

- elephant
- lion
- tiger
- giraffe
- monkey
- zebra
- hippo
- frog
- gorilla
- beetle

a	b	h	i	p	p	o	n	b	m	o	c
m	u	z	g	h	j	m	v	e	y	z	s
t	c	n	r	g	n	b	f	e	m	e	h
i	k	t	o	w	e	e	j	t	g	b	e
g	i	r	a	f	f	e	m	l	o	r	l
e	t	f	k	r	b	b	u	e	r	a	l
r	e	w	m	o	n	k	e	y	i	c	i
e	s	u	n	g	u	e	a	m	l	h	o
l	o	m	s	t	y	d	t	u	l	m	n
z	n	h	i	p	p	o	e	t	a	l	d
r	p	k	o	e	m	l	r	e	c	e	s
a	e	l	e	p	h	a	n	t	e	h	b

Silly animals

Q: Can a kangaroo jump higher than a mountain?
A: Of course. A mountain can't jump.

Q: What do you call a pig thief?
A: A hamburglar.

Q: How do you count cows?
A: With a cowculator.

Find the fish

Help the pelican find another fish. Make sure you avoid the heron or he'll get there first!

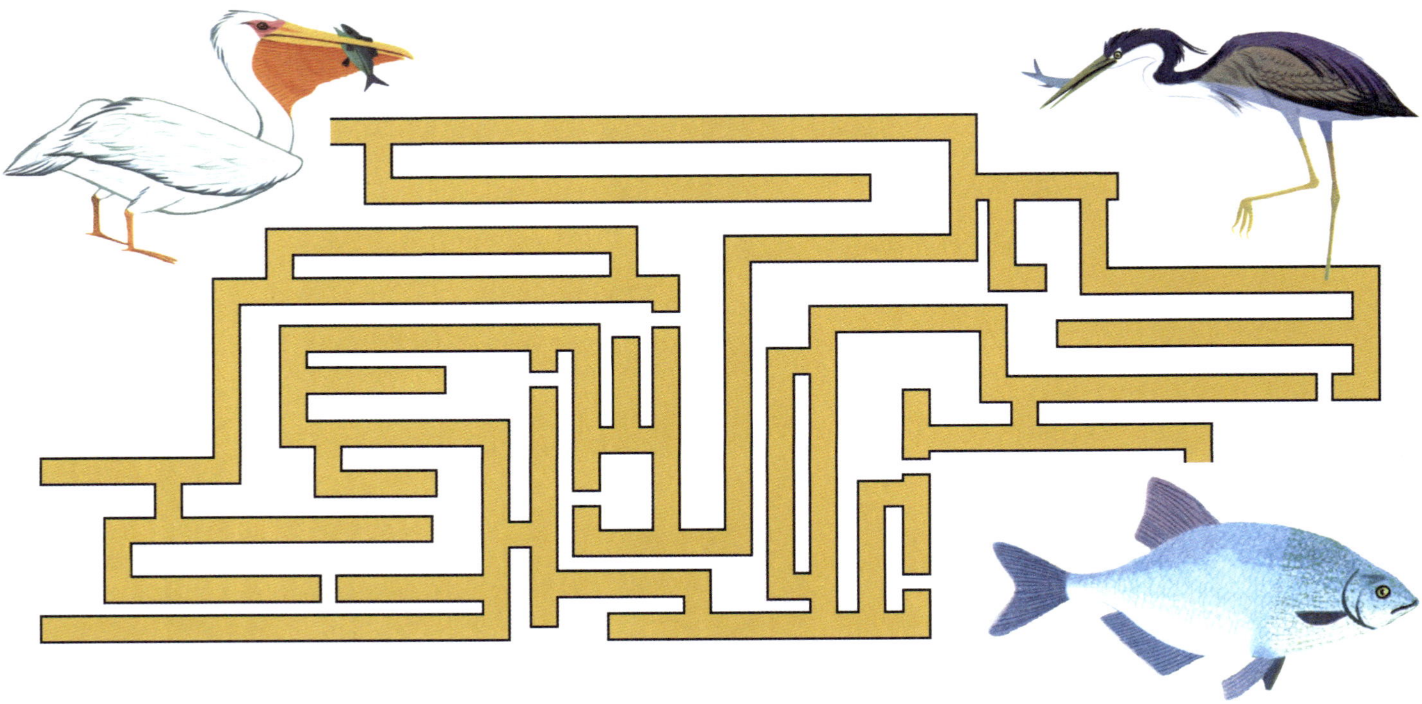

Underwater swimmers

Colour in these fish. How many fish can you count?

Spot the difference

Can you find five differences between these riverbank scenes?

Eggs in the basket

How many eggs has this chicken laid? Can you spot which one is about to hatch?

Sheep sticker fun

Add in some more sheep then help the shepherd and his dog count them. Don't fall asleep!

Count it up

Help the duck do his maths homework.

Bird of prey

Draw around the outline to complete the picture of this flying eagle. Then colour it in.

hatched	eggs	discover	strange
river	swan	ugly	reflection
cakes	shouted	fastest	raced
plodded	rest	tired	find
mother	white	pizza	ambled

Find the honey

Help the bee find the pot of honey.
He needs to stop off and gather nectar
from all the flowers along the way.

Greedy pig

Which pig has eaten all the food in his sty? He's got five black spots on his ecrs and two large black spots on his body.

Snack attack

These two crocodiles are hungry. But which one is going to get a juicy frog for its lunch?

Hairy lion

This lion wants to see what he looks like in the mirror as he might need a haircut! Can you draw around the outline to help and then colour him in?

Night owl

Colour in the birds so the owl can see them. How many stars can you count?

Weigh it up

These birds want to balance the scales. Can you help by putting two weights ir each tray so when they are added together it gives the same answer on both sides?

Farm sticker fun

Add in some birds and farm animals to make a busy farmyard scene.

Underwater maze

Can you help the diver find a path through the fish to reach the pink ones?

Linking lizard

Join the dots to complete the lizard, then colour it in.

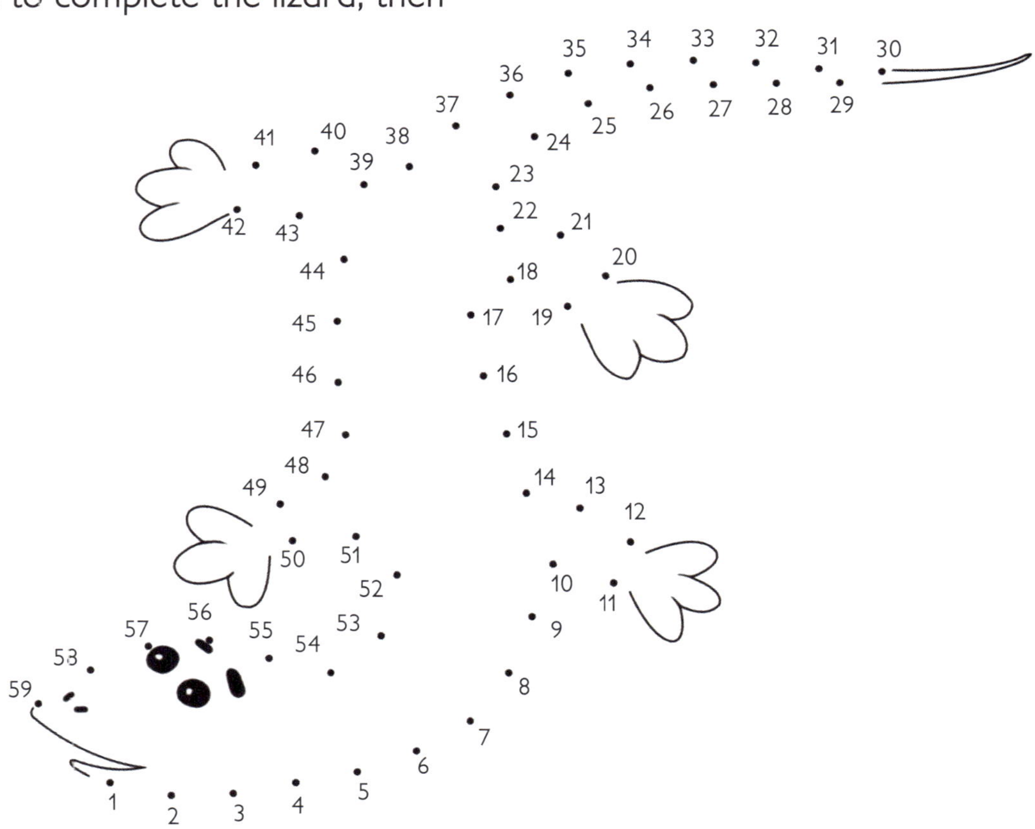

Vanishing fish

Help these fish reappear by matching the pattern of their scales, then colour them in.

Odd one out

Which of these crafty crabs is the odd one out?

Fishing tangle

Which fish are Polly and Jack going to catch?

Nutty hunt

Help the squirrel find the nuts she buried near the tree.

Snail surprise

Match the snail to the one on the rock.

Fishy dot to dot

Join the dots to see what this fish looks like, then colour him in.

Which of these animals...

have feathers? ____________________

have fur? ____________________

run on four legs? ____________________

Chicken

Bear

Duck

Dog

Parrot

Lion

Caterpillar maths

Help this cat measure the caterpillars by adding up the sums. Which one is the longest?

3 + 6 =

9 + 14 =

5 + 22 =

14 + 5 =

Who's in the box?

Unscramble the letters to find out which animal is in each box – choose from the lists and write in the white space. Then put stickers of them in the white space too.

bees
goats
snails
beetles
ducks

frogs
ants
horses
worms
dogs

Bee tangle

Which bee will reach the middle flower? Follow the tangled lines to find out.

Hungry frog

Help the frog jump through the flowers to the pond to reach his snack.
Make sure he avoids the hungry crocodiles on the way!

Jumping kangaroos

Which kangaroo can jump higher than the tree?

6+2+1=

4+3-2=

5+1+5=

2+3+2=

10 metres

Ant antics

How many different colours of ant are there? Put them in matching pairs by drawing a line between them.

Hungry bear

What do you think this bear likes to eat? Unscramble the letters to find out and write your answers in the boxes.

ajm

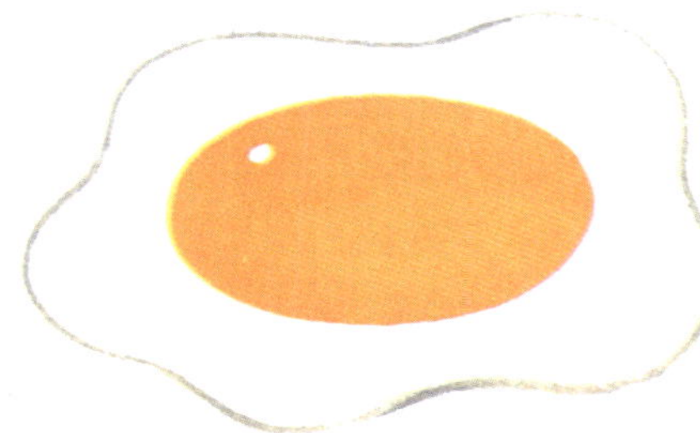

drefi geg

utns

eic arcem

eyohn

Funny fish

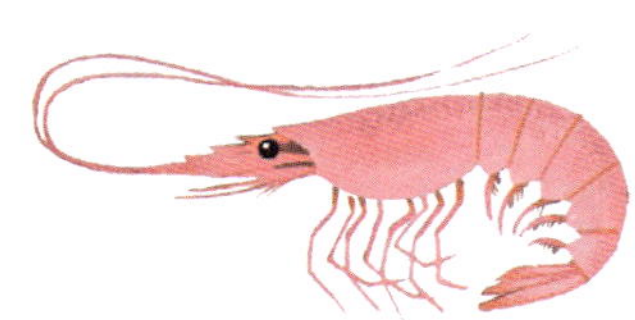

Q: Why didn't the prawn share his toys?
A: He was a little shellfish.

Q: What do fish eat to stay healthy?
A: Vitamin sea.

Q: What fish goes out at night?
A: A starfish.

Egg maths

Work out the sums. The batch of eggs with the highest number will hatch first.

Find the fruit

Which fruit will the bird eat? Follow the tangled lines to find out.

The ugly duckling

Choose words from the sticker pages to finish this story.

A mother duck sat on ten ______. Soon, they all ______. Nine ducklings looked just like their ______. The tenth was big and ______. All the other ducklings made fun of him. "Why are you so ______?" they cried. The poor duckling ran away to a ______ nearby, where he saw lots of beautiful white swans. "I wish I looked like them," he sighed. The duckling spent the winter by the river. In the spring, he looked at his ______ in the water and saw that he was a beautiful ______ too!

How many legs?

Which octopus has the right number of legs? See if you can draw another octopus with the right number of legs too.

Name game

Unscramble the names of the animals you can see. Add some animal stickers that you like to these pages. You can also draw some pictures of animals too.

dota

terfbuytl

gehodegh

gayrnoldf

ilasn

bldiryad

azilrd

hebenoye

bdri

Gorgeous giraffe

Finish drawing in the pattern on this giraffe and then colour him in.

Jumbled up

The kitten has got this wool all tangled up. Can you help her unravel it?

Ant maze

Polly and Jack want to help the ant find its way back to all the eggs. Can you help too? How many eggs can you count?

Little to large

Put these sea creatures in order of size, from smallest to largest.

Log carrier

How many logs does the elephant have to pick up, including the one already in his trunk?

Spot the difference

Can you spot five differences between these two pictures?

Car crazy

How many animals have hitched a lift?

Colour in the car to complete the picture.

Flower fun (page 2)

Down at the farm (page 6)

a	b	a	l	m	e	r	c	f	h	f	x
m	t	t	g	h	o	r	s	e	e	q	r
p	b	u	l	l	n	l	f	s	n	u	a
i	j	r	o	h	q	g	j	t	y	d	b
g	n	k	c	i	y	u	m	r	p	o	b
l	g	e	o	c	b	v	u	o	h	n	i
e	m	y	w	k	k	t	n	n	w	k	t
t	o	u	t	s	h	e	e	p	n	e	h
y	l	m	s	t	y	n	m	u	s	y	i
z	n	d	x	l	p	a	u	t	i	l	d
r	p	k	o	e	m	l	o	e	c	e	s
m	g	o	a	t	s	p	w	h	d	h	b

Spot the difference (page 3)

Hunt the chicks (page 6)

Monkey business (page 3)

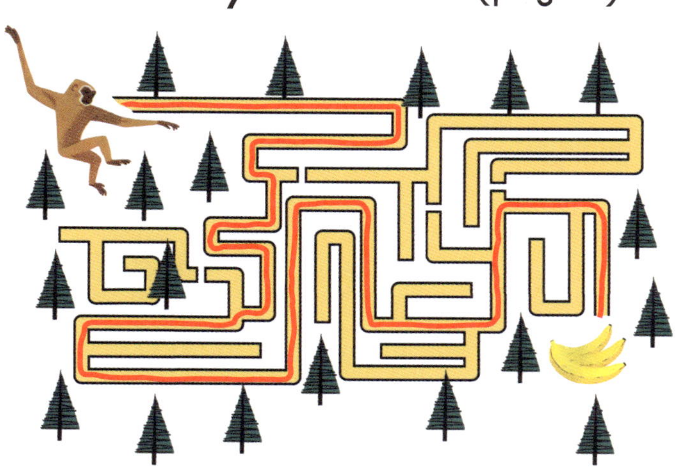

Bird buddies (page 7)

Gone fishing (page 8)

Find the eggs (page 12)

4 eggs

Odd one out (page 12)

Animal counting (page 12)

6 2 5 10 3

9 4 8 1 7

Total = 55

Hidden insects (page 14)

Animal quackers (page 14)

3 yellow 3 white 21 ducks in total

Jump start (page 18)

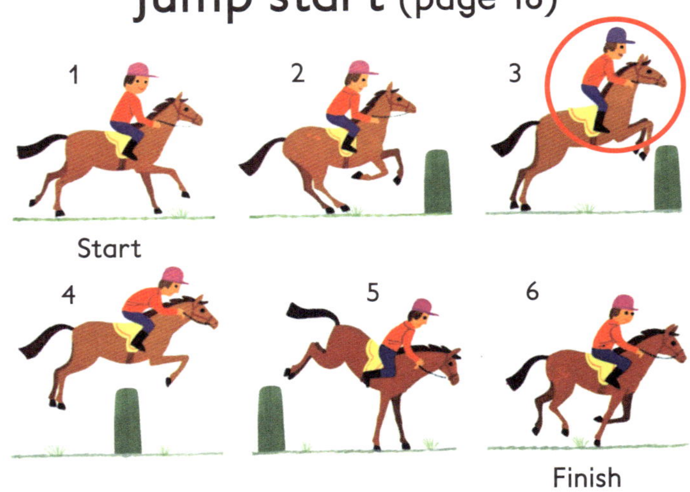

Find the hens (page 19)

Spot the difference (page 19)

Off on holiday (page 20)

Parasol
Fishing net
Spade
Rubber ring
Shirts
Flipper
Book
Towels
Rug
Bucket

Fishy friends (page 20)

s	a	s	h	a	r	k	w	n	m	m	o
w	m	u	z	g	h	j	m	v	a	t	t
o	s	a	l	m	o	n	p	p	c	m	r
r	o	k	m	o	a	q	t	j	k	y	o
d	l	e	w	c	l	y	u	m	e	p	u
f	e	t	f	o	m	b	n	u	r	h	t
i	t	m	v	d	o	k	a	n	e	w	c
s	e	g	u	p	p	y	e	a	l	n	h
h	y	o	m	s	t	y	n	m	u	s	m
z	n	d	x	l	p	a	c	a	r	p	d

All muddled up (page 23)

toga
GOAT

okoranag
KANGAROO

macel
CAMEL

tuvlure
VULTURE

Tangled lines (page 23)

Forest friends (page 24)

Owl, fox, wolf, rabbit, badger, squirrel, deer, rat, bluebird, tortoise, boar, pheasant.

Slowest animal: tortoise

Jungle pals (page 27)

a	b	h	i	p	p	o	n	b	m	o	c
m	u	z	g	h	j	m	v	e	y	z	s
t	c	n	r	g	n	b	f	e	m	e	h
i	k	t	o	w	e	e	j	t	g	b	e
g	i	r	a	f	f	e	m	l	o	r	l
e	t	f	k	r	b	b	u	e	r	a	l
r	e	w	m	o	n	k	e	y	i	c	i
e	s	u	n	g	u	e	a	m	l	h	o
l	o	m	s	t	y	d	t	u	l	m	n
z	n	h	i	p	p	o	e	t	a	l	d
r	p	k	o	e	m	l	r	e	c	e	s
a	e	l	e	p	h	a	n	t	e	h	b

Find the fish (page 28)

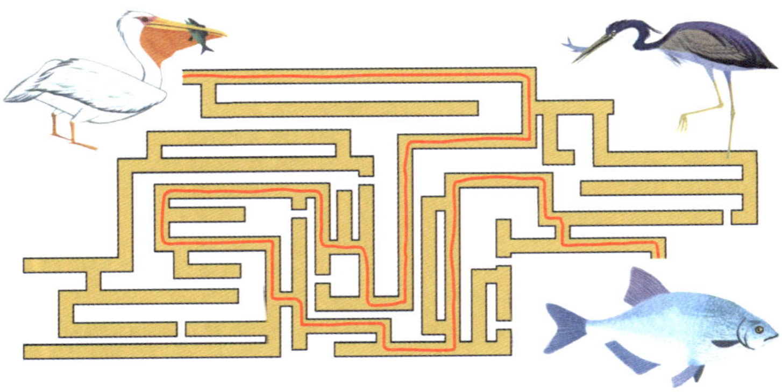

Find the honey (page 33)

Underwater swimmers (page 28)

How many fish? 8 fish

Greedy pig (page 33)

Spot the difference (page 29)

Snack attack (page 34)

Eggs in the basket (page 29)

16 eggs
in total

Night owl (page 35)

How many stars? 12 stars

Count it up (page 32)

Weigh it up (page 35)

Underwater maze (page 38)

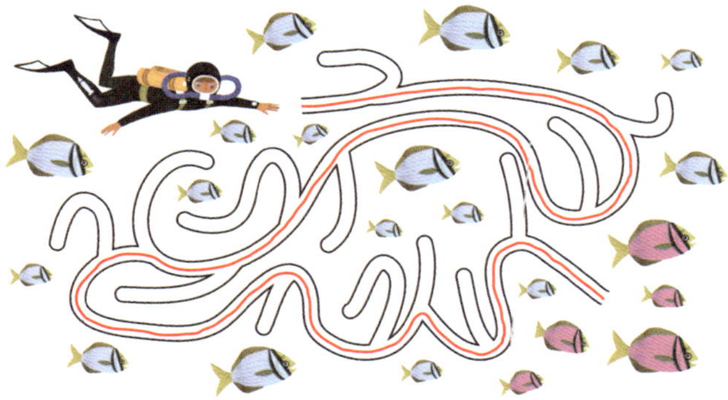

Odd one out (page 39)

Fishing tangle (page 40)

Nutty hunt (page 41)

Snail surprise (page 41)

Which animals... (page 43)

have feathers? Chicken, Duck, Parrot
have fur? Dog, Bear, Lion
run on all fours? Dog, Bear, Lion

Caterpillar maths (page 43)

3+6=9 9+14=23

5+22=27 14+5=19

Who's in the box? (page 44)

sebe = bees
snat = ants
msowr = worms
sorgf = frogs
sanils = snails

Bee tangle (page 45)

Hungry frog (page 45)

Egg maths (page 48)

Jumping kangaroos (page 46)

Find the fruit (page 48)

Ant antics (page 46)

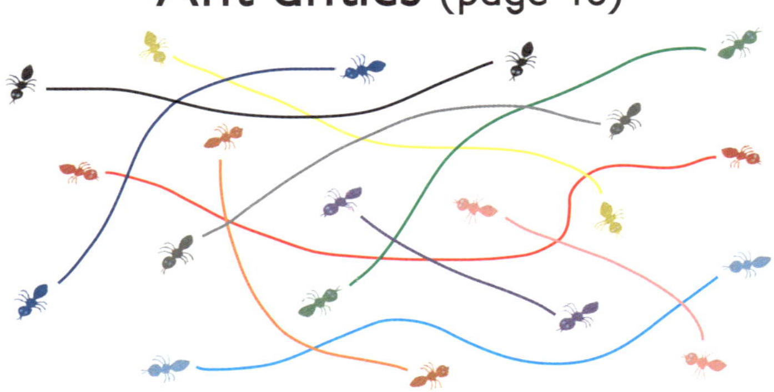

=9 different colours

How many legs? (page 49)

Hungry bear (page 47)

Name game (page 50)

toad
butterfly
hedgehog
dragonfly
snail
ladybird
lizard
honeybee
bird

Jumbled up (page 53)

Ant maze (page 53)

=8 eggs

Little to large (page 54)

Log carrier (page 54)

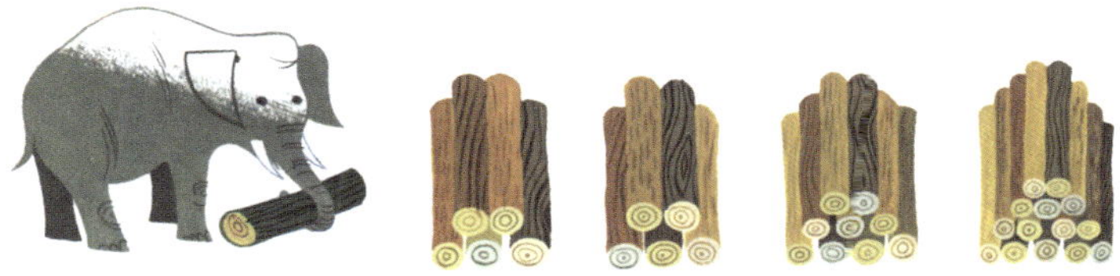

=34 logs

Spot the difference (page 55)

Car crazy (page 56)

12 animals: owl, cow, donkey, tortoise, penguin, dog, bear, duck, cat, crocodile, mouse and ladybird.

First published 2018 by Button Books, an imprint of Guild of Master Craftsman Publications Ltd, Castle Place, 166 High Street, Lewes, East Sussex BN7 1XU, UK. Text © GMC Publications Ltd, 2018. Copyright in the Work © GMC Publications Ltd, 2018. Illustrations © 2018 A.G. & RicoBel. ISBN 978 1 78708 018 8. All rights reserved. The right of Alain Grée to be identified as the illustrator of this work has been asserted in accordance with the Copyright, Designs and Patents Act 1988, sections 77 and 78. No part of this publication may be reproduced, stored in a retrieval system or transmitted in any form or by any means without the prior permission of the publisher and copyright owner. While every effort has been made to obtain permission from the copyright holders for all material used in this book, the publishers will be pleased to hear from anyone who has not been appropriately acknowledged and to make the correction in future reprints. The publishers and author can accept no legal responsibility for any consequences arising from the application of information, advice or instructions given in this publication. A catalogue record for this book is available from the British Library. Publisher: Jonathan Bailey. Production: Jim Bulley, Jo Pallett. Senior Project Editor: Sara Harper. Managing Art Editor: Gilda Pacitti. Designer: Alex Bailey. Colour origination by GMC Reprographics. Printed and bound in China. Warning! Choking hazard – small parts. Not suitable for children under 3 years.